stitches

Stitchapalooza!

Introduction	5
Straight Stitches	6
Diagonal Stitches	17
Multi Layered Stitches	26
Borders and Backgrounds	33
Embroidery and Embellishment	46
Index	54

As I write this introduction for Book Four in our Got Stitches series, the world has had a tough couple of years. We shut ourselves in and coped the best we knew how. Stitchers took to the safety of their needles and canvases, trying to stitch the pandemic away. But as we slowly emerged, completed projects in tow, we began to reconnect with our stitching friends and shops. Here at Gone Stitching we learned new ways to bring people together to stitch, talk and just have fun. We think its time for a party! Time to mix things up, learn new stitches and techniques, and take some chances.

So we propose,
Stitchapalooza:
a wild, crazy, & extravagant stitching party!

Pull yourselves out of your stitching rut by turning the page to a new stitch you've never tried. Go ahead, make some mistakes, pull it out and do it again. We have included new sections in this book including **Embroidery and Embellishment** and **Borders and Backgrounds** to make your projects shine. So grab your needle, pour yourself your favorite drink and join us at the Stitchapalooza - LET THE PARTY BEGIN!

Happy Stitching!

Michele and Renée

The Gone Stitching Gals

Straight Stitches

Bargello Arch

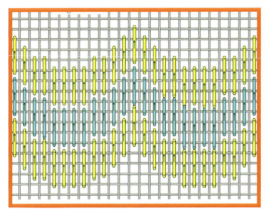

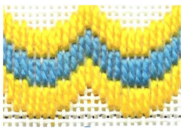

Bargello Ribbons

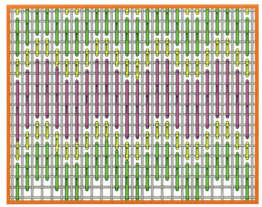

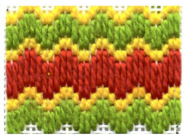

Stitchapalooza!

Bargello Pavillion Diamonds

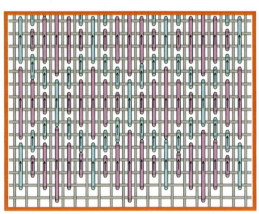

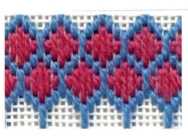

Simple Bargello

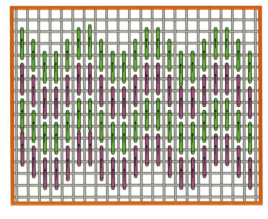

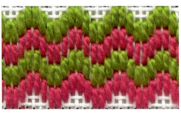

Straight Stitches

Barred Beetle

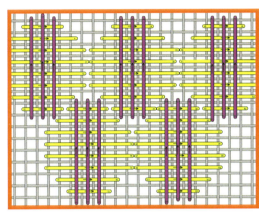
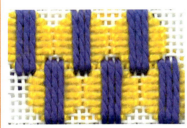

Cascading Stripe

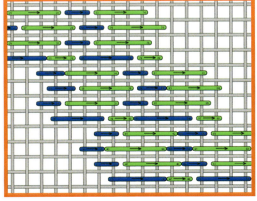
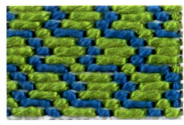

Stitchapalooza!

Flemish Bond

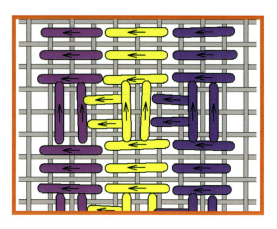

Folding Twill

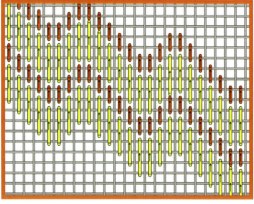

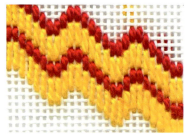

11

Straight Stitches

Gobelin Bars With Tent

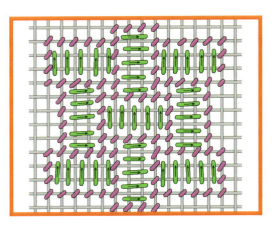

Inverted Scallops

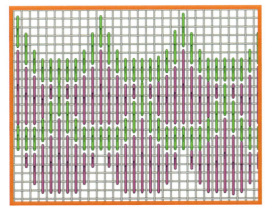

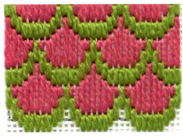

Vertical Jacquard

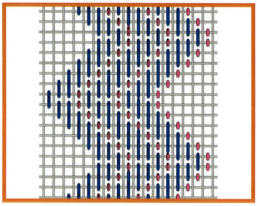

Fence Stitch

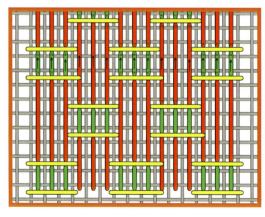

Straight Stitches

Linen Fold

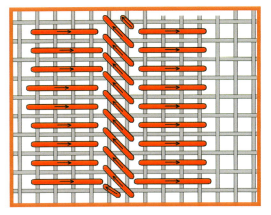

Milanese Mirror

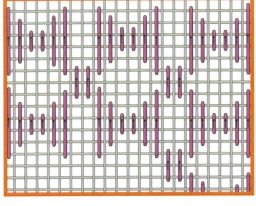
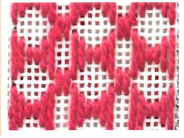

Stitchapalooza!

Horizontal Old Florentine

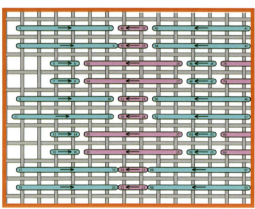

Horizontal Oriental

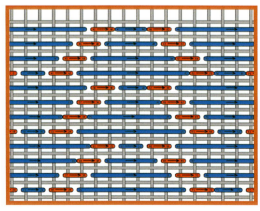
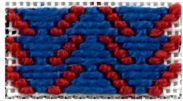

Straight Stitches

15

Offset Double Twill

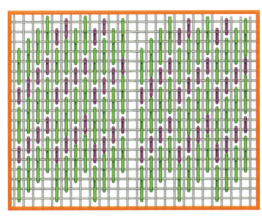 

Patterned 3

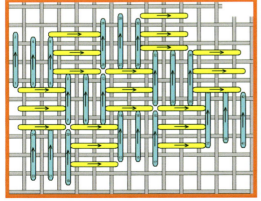 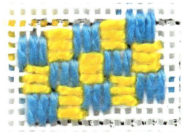

Wheat Sheaf

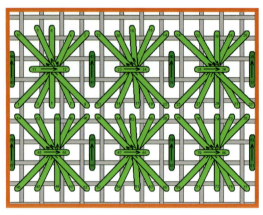

Checkerboard Cross

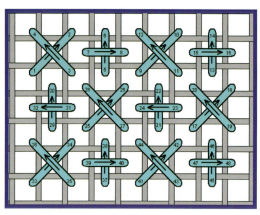
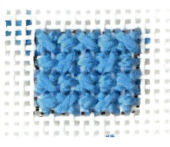

Dutch

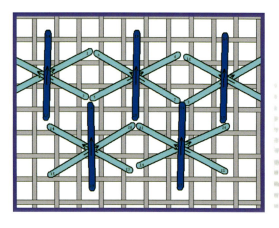

Diagonal Stitches

Vertical Beaty

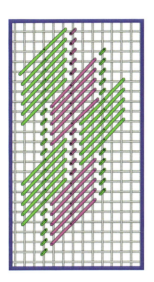 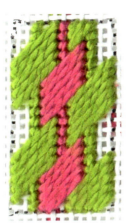

Diagonal Wave

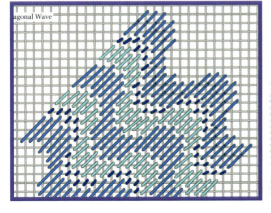 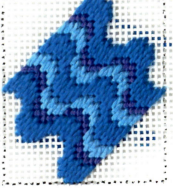

Betsy

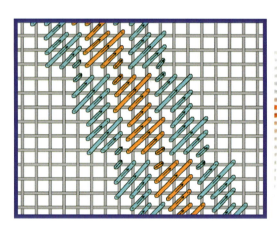
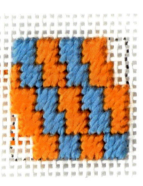

Diagonal Cashmere

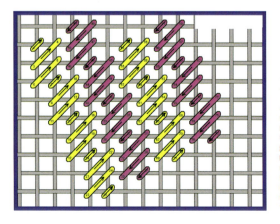

Diagonal Stitches

Chutes and Ladders

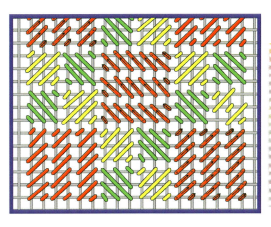

Encroaching Gobelin

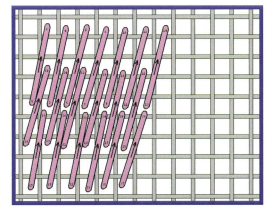

Hesitation Stitch

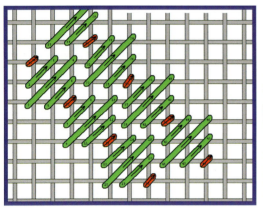
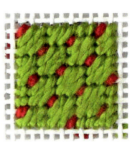

Keenan

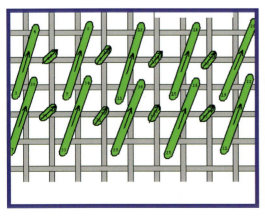

Diagonal Stitches

Milanese

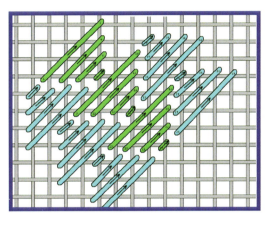

Moorish

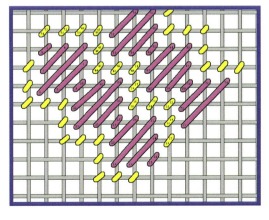

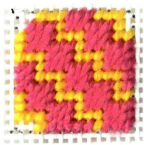

Oriental

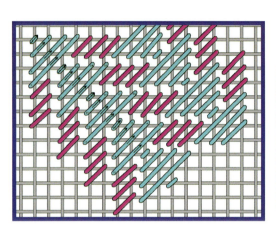
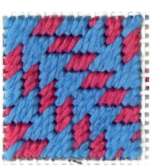

Diagonal Pavillion

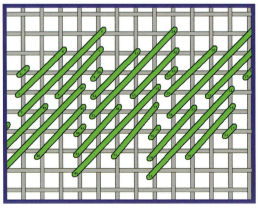

Diagonal Stitches

Snow Storm

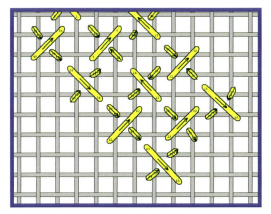

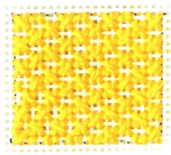

Multi Layered Stitches

Candy Platter Stitch

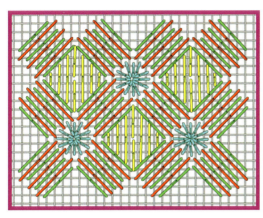
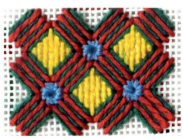

Circular Swirl

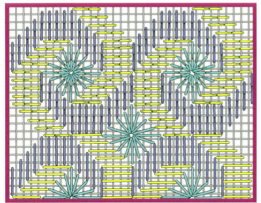

Squareburst

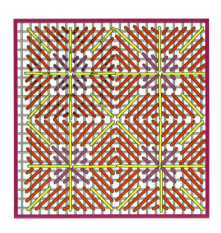

Squareburst with Diamond

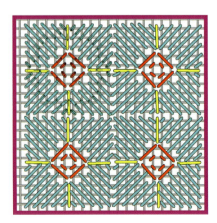
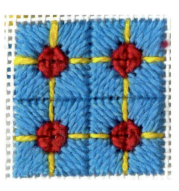

Multi Layered Stitches

Circleburst

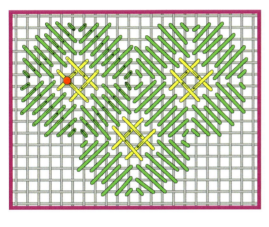

Flying Dumbells

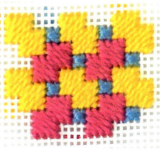

Large Diamond Hungarian

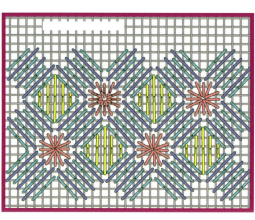

Kimi

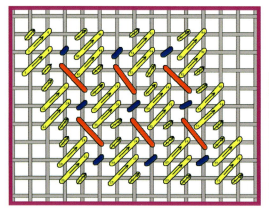
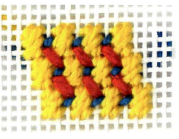

Multi Layered Stitches

Lozenge Stitch

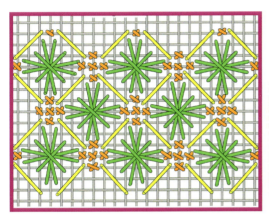

Pavillion Boxes

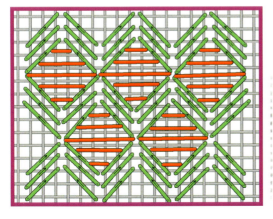

Stitchapalooza!

Pavillion Steps

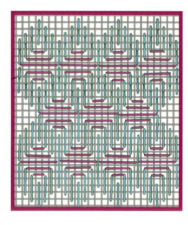

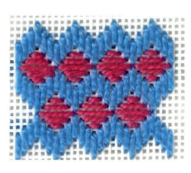

Ka-Boom!

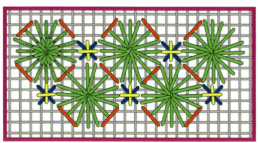

Stitchapalooza!

Bundle-O-Sticks Border

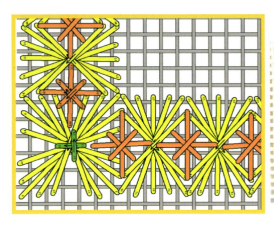
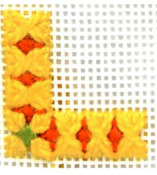

Tangled & Tied Border Over 8

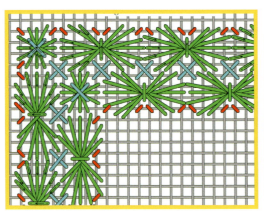

Borders and Backgrounds

35

Chain Link

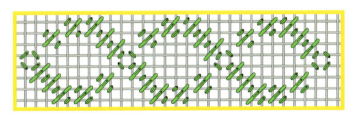

Balloon Darning Pattern

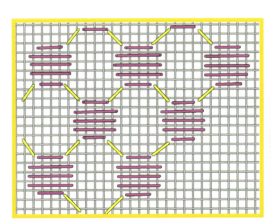

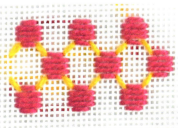

Braided Stripe

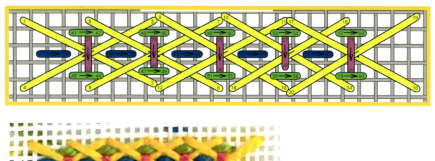

Large Crossed Diamond Border w/ 2 options

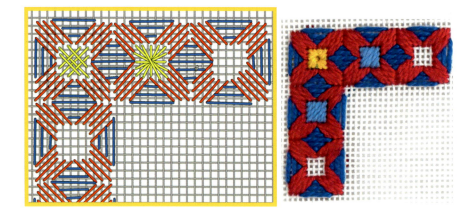

Borders and Backgrounds

Brick Darning Pattern

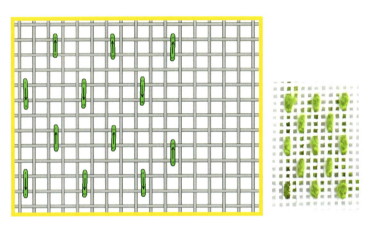

Diamond Darning

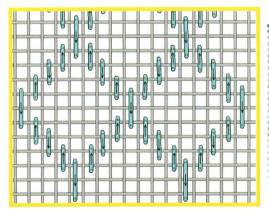

Dreidel Darning

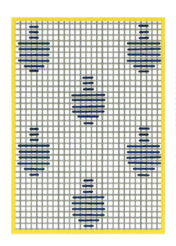
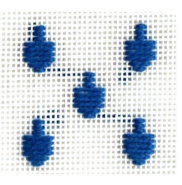

Laid Alternating Cross Darning Pattern

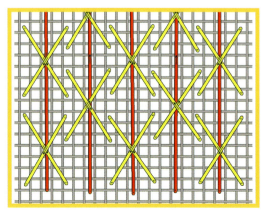
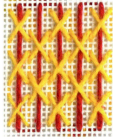

Borders and Backgrounds

Fish Darning

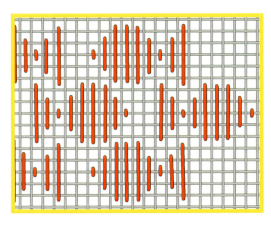

Flying Leaflets

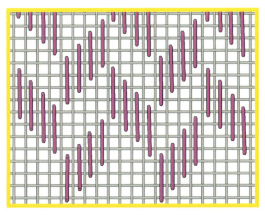

Heart Darning

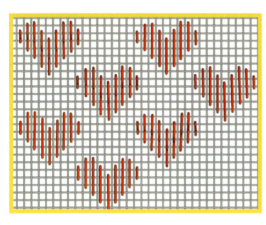

Layered Smyrna Border

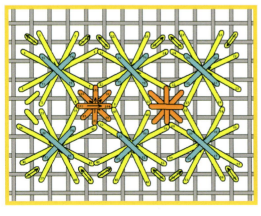
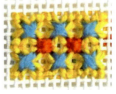

Borders and Backgrounds

Menorah Darning

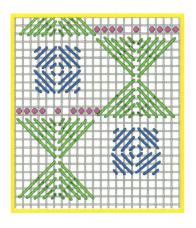
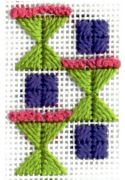

Oblique Crossed Corner Border

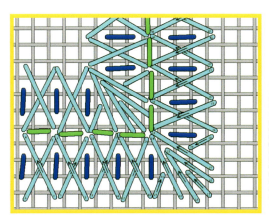
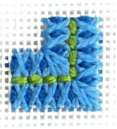

Open Double Woven

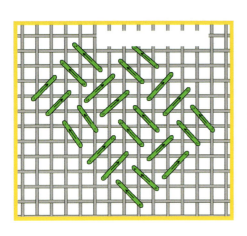

Ping Pong Balls Darning

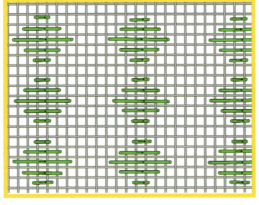

Borders and Backgrounds

Pots and Pans Darning

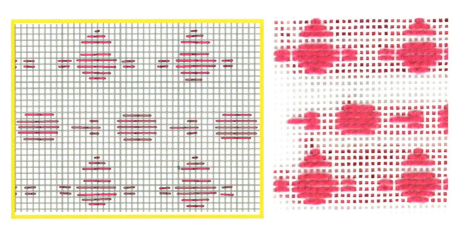

Tied Crossed Border

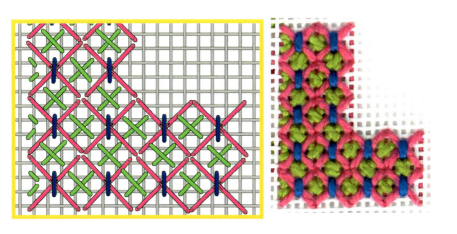

Triple Delight Darning

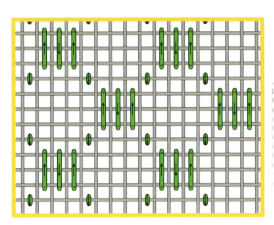
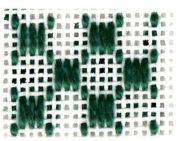

Vine Darning

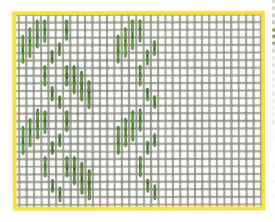

Borders and Backgrounds

Wine Glass Darning

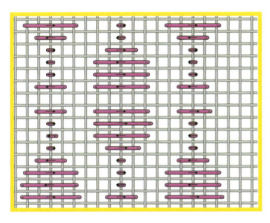

Embroidery and Embellishment

47

Chain

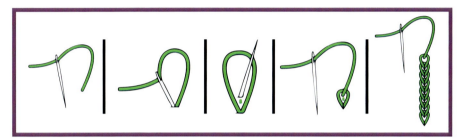

Free Form Fly

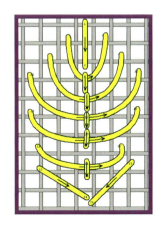

Stitchapalooza!

French Knot

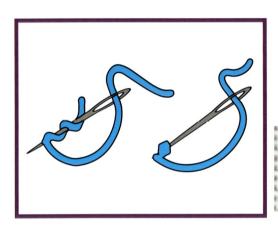

French Knot On A Stalk

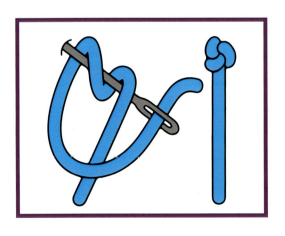

Embroidery and Embellishment

Ribbon Rose

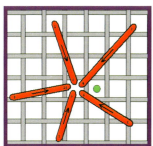

1. Make 5 even stitches, all into the same hole.
2. Bring your needle up near the center of one of the spokes, but not in the center (see green dot on diagram)
3. Weave your thread over the first spoke, then under the second, over the third and so on.
4. Continue weaving until all of the spokes are covered.
5. The tighter you pull, the more raised the rose will look.
6. For a larger rose, use 7 spokes as your base.

Stem Stitch

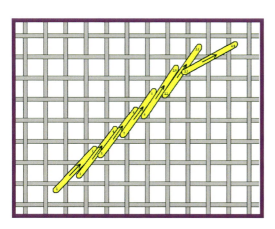

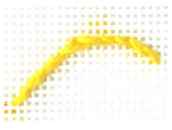

Stitchapalooza!

Whipped Back Stitch

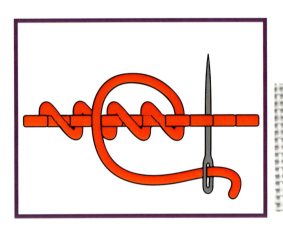
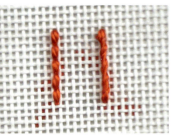

Bricked Turkey Work

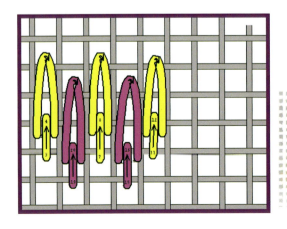

Embroidery and Embellishment

51

Covered Washers

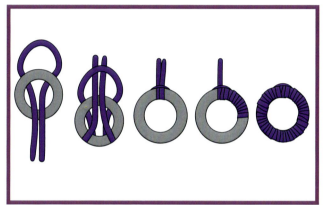

Messy Beading

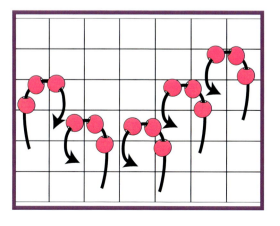

Stitchapalooza!

Brick Style Beading

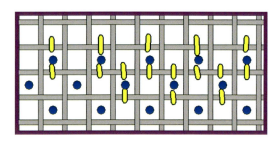

Basketweave Beading

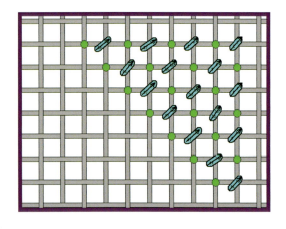

Embroidery and Embellishment

Long and Short

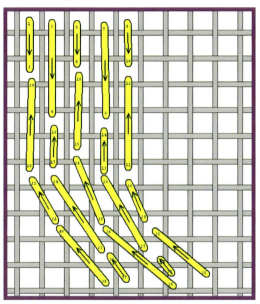

Bullion Knot

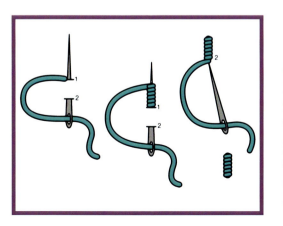

Index

Stitch Name	Stitch Type	Difficulty Level	Page
Balloon Darning Pattern	Border & Background	intricate	35
Bargello Arch	Straight	simple	7
Bargello Pavillion Diamonds	Straight	moderate	8
Bargello Ribbons	Straight	moderate	7
Barred Beetle	Straight	simple	9
Basketweave Beading	Embroidery & Embellishment	moderate	52
Betsy	Diagonal	moderate	20
Braided Stripe	Border & Background	intricate	36
Brick Darning Pattern	Border & Background	moderate	37
Brick Style Beading	Embroidery & Embellishment	moderate	52
Bricked Turkey Work	Embroidery & Embellishment	moderate	50
Bullion Knot	Embroidery & Embellishment	intricate	53
Bundle-O-Sticks Border	Border & Background	intricate	34
Candy Platter Stitch	Multi Layered	intricate	27
Cascading Stripe	Straight	moderate	9
Chain	Embroidery & Embellishment	simple	47
Chain Link	Border & Background	intricate	35
Checkerboard Cross	Diagonal	simple	18
Chutes and Ladders	Diagonal	intricate	21
Circleburst	Multi Layered	intricate	29
Circular Swirl	Multi Layered	intricate	27
Covered Washers	Embroidery & Embellishment	simple	51
Diagonal Cashmere	Diagonal	simple	20
Diagonal Pavillion	Diagonal	simple	24
Diagonal Wave	Diagonal	intricate	19
Diamond Darning	Border & Background	moderate	37
Dreidel Darning	Border & Background	moderate	38
Dutch	Diagonal	simple	18
Encroaching Gobelin	Diagonal	simple	21

Stitchapalooza!

Stitch Name	Stitch Type	Difficulty Level	Page
Fence Stitch	Straight	moderate	12
Fish Darning	Border & Background	moderate	39
Flemish Bond	Straight	simple	10
Flying Dumbells	Multi Layered	intricate	29
Flying Leaflets	Border & Background	moderate	39
Folding Twill	Straight	simple	10
Free Form Fly	Embroidery & Embellishment	moderate	47
French Knot	Embroidery & Embellishment	simple	48
French Knot On A Stalk	Embroidery & Embellishment	moderate	48
Gobelin Bars With Tent	Straight	intricate	11
Heart Darning	Border & Background	moderate	40
Hesitation Stitch	Diagonal	moderate	22
Horizontal Old Florentine	Straight	simple	14
Horizontal Oriental	Straight	simple	14
Inverted Scallops	Straight	simple	11
Ka-Boom!	Multi Layered	intricate	32
Keenan	Diagonal	simple	22
Kimi	Multi Layered	intricate	30
Laid Alternating Cross Darning Pattern	Border & Background	moderate	38
Large Crossed Diamond Border w/ 2 options	Border & Background	intricate	36
Large Diamond Hungarian	Multi Layered	intricate	30
Layered Smyrna Border	Border & Background	intricate	40
Linen Fold	Straight	simple	13
Long and Short	Embroidery & Embellishment	moderate	53
Lozenge Stitch	Multi Layered	intricate	31
Menorah Darning	Border & Background	intricate	41
Messy Beading	Embroidery & Embellishment	simple	51

Index

Stitch Name	Stitch Type	Difficultly Level	Page
Milanese	Diagonal	simple	23
Milanese Mirror	Straight	simple	13
Moorish	Diagonal	moderate	23
Oblique Crossed Corner Border	Border & Background	intricate	41
Offset Double Twill	Straight	moderate	15
Open Double Woven	Border & Background	moderate	42
Oriental	Diagonal	moderate	24
Patterned 3	Straight	moderate	15
Pavillion Boxes	Multi Layered	moderate	31
Pavillion Steps	Multi Layered	moderate	32
Ping Pong Balls Darning	Border & Background	simple	42
Pots and Pans Darning	Border & Background	intricate	43
Ribbon Rose	Embroidery & Embellishment	simple	49
Simple Bargello	Straight	simple	8
Snow Storm	Diagonal	moderate	25
Squareburst	Multi Layered	intricate	28
Squareburst with Diamond	Multi Layered	intricate	28
Stem Stitch	Embroidery & Embellishment	simple	49
Tangled and Tied Border over 8	Border & Background	intricate	34
Tied Crossed Border	Border & Background	intricate	43
Triple Delight Darning	Border & Background	moderate	44
Vertical Beaty	Diagonal	simple	19
Vertical Jacquard	Straight	moderate	12
Vine Darning	Border & Background	intricate	44
Wheat Sheaf	Straight	intricate	16
Whipped Back Stitch	Embroidery & Embellishment	simple	50
Wine Glass Darning	Border & Background	moderate	45

Notes